The Pendulum SWINGS BACK

Stories from When We Almost Lost Everything

Sugar Gay Isber McMillan

The Pendulum Swings Back

The Pendulum *Swings* Back
Stories from When
We Almost Lost Everything

Copyright © 2026 by Sugar Gay Isber McMillan
All rights reserved.

This book is a work of fiction. Names, characters, places, events, and incidents are either the product of the author's imagination or used fictitiously. Any resemblance to actual persons, living or dead, or to real events is purely coincidental.

No part of this book may be reproduced, stored in a retrieval system, or transmitted in any form or by any means without the prior written permission of the publisher, except for brief quotations in reviews.

ISBN: 978-1-967973-86-6

Published by
The WOW Book Co.™

Printed in the United States of America

Large font edition.

The Pendulum Swings Back

Recorder's Note

The accounts in this book were collected over time, in no fixed order, and under no uniform conditions.

Some were spoken in kitchens. Some in cars. Some while walking. Some after long silences. Some arrived in fragments, returned to later, corrected, contradicted, or left unresolved.

Not every voice could be verified.
Not every name could be kept.
Not every detail could be confirmed without endangering the person who shared it.

Where possible, voices were preserved as they were given. Grammar was not standardized unless clarity required it. Contradictions were not resolved unless the speaker resolved them. Gaps were left intact.

This book does not attempt to determine guilt or innocence. It does not establish timelines beyond what the speakers themselves provided. It does not claim completeness.

Some stories end abruptly because that is how they were given.

Some never end at all.

The recorder did not witness the events described. The recorder did not adjudicate them. The recorder listened, recorded, and preserved.

Silence is part of the record.

Absence is part of the record.

What is missing from this book is as deliberate as what remains.

What This Book Is Not

This book is not an investigation.
It's not a legal brief.
It's not a policy proposal.
It's not a comprehensive history.

It does not offer solutions.
It does not assign sentences.
It does not reconcile competing truths.

This book does not claim neutrality.
It also does not claim authority.

It's not written to persuade, to comfort, or to entertain. It does not seek consensus, closure, or catharsis.

The voices gathered here are not representative. They are not proportional. They are not balanced.

They are present.

This book does not argue that what happened was inevitable.
It does not argue that what happened is finished.

It records what people say they lived through, after the moment when speaking again became possible.

If this book leaves questions unanswered, that is intentional.
If it feels incomplete, that reflects the record itself.

Nothing here is meant to stand alone.
Nothing here asks to be the final word.

The Pendulum Swings Back

Table of Contents

RECORDER'S NOTE 3

THIS BOOK IS NOT 5

CHAPTER 1 11

ICE AGENT
Midwestern United States
Employed by Immigration Enforcement

CHAPTER 2 19

BANK TELLER
Oklahoma
Detained after an internal inquiry

CHAPTER 3 29

ELEMENTARY SCHOOL TEACHER
NOT DETAINED BUT WANTED TO LEAVE A STATEMENT
New Jersey

CHAPTER 4 35

NURSING HOME WORKER
Explaining The Purge
Utah

CHAPTER 5 39

ER DOCTOR
WHAT IT WAS LIKE
Chicago

CHAPTER 6 46

RANCHER IN TEXAS

VACCINATING CATTLE

CHAPTER 7 50

HISTORY PROFESSOR
PASSPORT VIOLATION
St. Louis

CHAPTER 8 57

UNATTRIBUTED STATEMENT

(recorded without identifiers, location withheld)

CHAPTER 9 61

The Plumber
Texas

CHAPTER 10 72

Military Man
No NAME GIVEN
No location allowed

CHAPTER 11 78

Eleven-Year-Old Boy
Birmingham, Mississippi

CHAPTER 12 80

THE INFLUENCER
SOCIAL MEDIA CRIMES
Louisianna

CHAPTER 13 91

Teenage Girl
Arizona

CHAPTER 14 96

SWITCH TECHNICIAN
California

CHAPTER 15 100

THE STUDDER
(He wanted to be recorded
Utah

CHAPTER 16 105

MAIL CARRIER
Washington State

CHAPTER 17 111

Imprisoned for Rioting
Portland, Maine

CHAPTER 18 117

Alabama Preacher
Imprisoned for Domestic Terrorism

CHAPTER 19 123

COMMERCIAL REAL ESTATE AGENT
Atlanta, Georgia
Detained for not having her passport

CHAPTER 20 135

No Passport Violation
West Virginia

CHAPTER 21 140

No Passport Violation
West Virginia

CHAPTER 22 143

Clerk, Intake Division
PHILADELPHIA

CHAPTER 23 145

Accountant
Colorado

FINAL NOTE 152

ABOUT THE AUTHOR 153

CHAPTER 1

ICE AGENT

Midwestern United States
Employed by Immigration Enforcement

I don't really want to talk.
My mother always said, just be quiet.

But I think I need to say this.
If you're writing it down, fine.
I want you to know what happened to me.
So you understand that we were all broken.

They dangled things in front of us.
Fame.
Glory.
Money.

None of it came true.
None of it.

But we got to wear the clothes.

I should back up.

My sophomore year in high school, my mother's husband, my dad, decided he was gay and left. Just left the house. Small town. Everyone knew.

The bullying came fast. They said I must be gay too. My mother was wrecked. I was wrecked.

That was the first crack.

I hated school. I always had. English especially. Reading. Writing. None of it mattered to me. My mother signed me up for summer school because I missed too much. She had to clock out of work every day to pick me up. She tried hard. She really did.

I lied.

She dropped me off with a sack lunch. The bullies watched. I ran. I came back at pickup time. Told her I got a B-plus. Said summer school was easier than real school.

At the fair, a teacher came up and said I wasn't there all summer. My mother screamed. Everyone heard. The bullies heard. That followed me.

Junior year. No future.

The military didn't appeal. Getting up early never did. College wasn't an option. My grades were bad. My scores were bad. My mother said I had three choices: college, military, or death.

I saw the ads. You saw them too. M-O-N-E-Y, they were making us think we would be rich. Purpose. Belonging. A uniform. A place to sleep.

My mother begged me not to go.

Two months later I was in it.

All the guys were the same. Either bullies or beaten. Angry either way. I wanted money. I needed a place to live. I needed something to belong to.

I didn't think too hard about it. You stop thinking.

I'd seen war movies. I knew what crying looked like. Begging. Hands up. I knew the sounds. I didn't know what it felt like to cause them.

At first I was scared. Then it felt powerful.

The click of the handcuffs was satisfying. I won't lie.
You roll them into the van and move on.

There were quotas. Numbers. Money on the table. If you didn't meet them, you fell back. If you met them, you got better assignments. Better gear.

They didn't tell you the money took five years.

I lasted longer than I thought I would.

I did terrible things. I will never tell my mother what I did.

It didn't feel like neighbors. Different city. Different faces. We had beds. Food. Weapons. They had floors.

One time I went where they were taken.

It was worse than I imagined.

We ate three meals. I don't know if they got water. They slept on concrete. No space. No quiet.

I went back to my room after.
Closed the door.
Laid down.

That part was easy.

Going back to the room.
Closing the door.
Doing it again the next day.

The hard part was the guys.

I'm not excusing me. I'm not excusing them. What we did was terrible. Some of them were worse than others. I wasn't one of the ones messing with the girls. I didn't care. The girls weren't my thing. Maybe boys weren't either. Maybe I just didn't know yet. Maybe at thirty I would've figured that out.

Back then it didn't matter.

Every day had a kind of high. Getting into the vans. Talking big. Talking trash. Acting like we were something. Macho. Loud. All of it.

Then we'd get out in full gear. Shields up. Buckets of piss. Balloons full of shit. People screaming. Things hitting you. You push through anyway.

That part was horrible.

I just wanted the paycheck.

There were too many of us. Way more than we needed. Sometimes I didn't even know what we were doing. We were picking at people because of skin color. That still doesn't sit right. I grew up around all kinds of people. Never thought about it. Then suddenly that was the job.

Smack people around. Handcuffs. Vans. Lock them up.

The day it ended, I wanted to cry.

They told us to take the uniforms off. Take your things. Don't leave anything personal. You're not coming back. Doors opened. That was it.

Go home.

I didn't even know how to get home. No help. No instructions. Just done.

They were never helpful. Not once.

The people I killed, it felt like self-defense. It felt like war. That's how it was framed. I didn't think about the big picture. Didn't think about how close we all really are. Six degrees and all that. We didn't talk about it that way.

We were told they were the enemy.

Every night they worked us up. Chanting. Screaming. Getting us angry. Then you try to sleep and you can't because your head is still loud.

I'll never tell my mother any of this.

I'm telling you because I want you to know why I joined. I joined because I was the target once. I knew that feeling. I wanted something easier. Something that didn't feel like shit rolling downhill all the time.

I don't want you to think everyone there was the same. We weren't. But there were about ten of us who wanted to hurt people. That surprised me. At the end of the day, I wanted it too. I wanted to see how it felt to kill someone.

After the first time, it got easier.

Maybe it was the movies. The games. All that war stuff we grew up on. I'm glad those are gone now.

There'll probably be movies about this time.

At least we didn't march like Nazis. They didn't care about discipline. They just wanted numbers. Grab someone. Van. Lunch. Repeat.

We filled one of the centers completely one day. We called them dog houses. We were awful. They gave us the next day off.

We went back to the hotel. Video games. Videos that were gross. Things that kept the energy ugly.

I'm sure they'll come for me. They say now some of what we did wasn't legal. They told us it was.

The judge says no cell phone. Fine. I don't need to call anyone.

I need a job. No one will hire me. I've got a tattoo on my forehead I regret. No money saved. They charged us for everything. Guns weren't free. Bullets weren't free. Tear gas wasn't free. They took it out of our pay.

If you picked up the wrong gear, you paid for it. Sometimes you paid with your body.

I'm glad it's over.

Things are quieter.

It's like the war ended. But not like in the movies, there was no one excited that we were ending.

I think it started when my dad left. When he said he was gay and walked out. I think that's where it broke. Not my mother. Him.

Then I turned into this.

I'll take whatever comes.

I don't know what's supposed to be good now.

Chapter 2

BANK TELLER
Oklahoma
Detained after an internal inquiry

I worked at a bank in Oklahoma for more than ten years. Born and raised there. That bank was good to me. I liked the hours. I liked getting dressed up. I liked the way people stood a little straighter when I told them where I worked, like their mortgage might be due and maybe I could help them.

I couldn't. But I smiled.

I'm half Mexican and half Indian. I look more Indian than Mexican. It never mattered much. My mama and my papa loved each other. They made love work in our family. They raised us right. We were happy kids. My daddy always said you get a job when you finish high school and you'll be good at something. He meant it. We all did it.

I liked being a banker. I worked my way up. It felt good to be part of an international institution. I won't say the name of the bank. They don't deserve it. They were part of the problem. I didn't see it at first. I only saw pieces.

I knew my customers. The ones who came in every two weeks with their paychecks. Mortgage. Insurance. Light bill. Water bill. Groceries. A little left over. Then they'd come back the next week, take some out, put some more in. I knew their names. Their kids. Who was graduating. Who had a wedding coming. That was the best part of my day.

So, when did I first see it going wrong?

Like everyone else, I was on social media. Yes, I was. I screamed my fair share. It let some of the rage out. There was always something to scream about. Every day brought a new shock. I don't even know how many years that went on. I wasn't doing anything bad. Recipes. Cleaning tips. Funny dogs. Just like everybody else. I wouldn't touch it now. I'm sure it's all backed up somewhere anyway.

The first thing was one of our tellers. She didn't come in one day. She was Hispanic. We had her passport on file. You can't work at a bank without proving who you are. Later, we heard she and her husband had been taken. We were never told where. I didn't believe it at first. None of us did. We left her drawer just the way it was. We thought she'd be back.

She never was.

Then customers stopped coming. Regular customers. People who didn't look any certain way. I never thought about what they were. They just stopped showing up. Those two-week checks disappeared. The rhythm of the place broke.

The real red flag came the day there was a demonstration outside the bank. Just a normal Tuesday. Everything was already upside down by then. Protests. Police. Sirens. Anger. Fear. Everybody saw it. I told my family not to worry. I said I worked at a bank. I'd be fine.

But if you weren't carrying your passport, if you didn't look exactly right, if your hair was dark, if you were a pretty woman, that could be enough.

They'd pull you over.

Where's your passport?

Why are you recording us?

Step out of the car, ma'am.

You didn't have to speed. You didn't have to mouth off. You didn't have to do anything. Sometimes it was just the way you looked that day.

I went back to work shaken. I knew I was being watched. I cut back on everything. I went straight home. I followed every rule.

Still, more people stopped coming in.

I watched the daily deposits fall. The bank felt hollow. And then I noticed something else. Big money coming in. Big deposits. From the customers who always demanded special treatment. The ones who reminded you they'd been with the bank forever.

That's when I started to understand.

That's when I began to understand there were two kinds of people banking with us.

There were the ones with regular jobs. Paychecks. Mortgages. Light bills. And then there were the others. The ones whose money moved without them ever stepping inside the building. The ones tied to millionaires, or who were millionaires themselves. The money just floated in and out. Checking accounts. Savings. Market accounts. Treasury bills. Ledgers on top of ledgers.

We could see it all. We weren't supposed to talk about it. We were trained not to. We knew exactly how much people were worth the moment their name came up. Some numbers could turn your stomach. That information stayed behind the glass. Always had.

Until it didn't make sense anymore.

All of a sudden, money started pouring in. Big money. No paperwork. No people standing at the counter. Just deposits appearing. Twenty million here. Five million there. I remember the first time I saw a transfer to the sheriff's account. I stared at the screen. Then another one went to a real estate executive. Then another. And another.

At the same time, our regular customers were disappearing.

People who had never missed a deposit. People whose routines I knew by heart. Gone.

I tried to make sense of it. I looked at it sideways. I asked myself why the richest people in town were getting richer overnight while the working people were vanishing. It didn't add up.

I asked a question.

It was on one of our Thursday management calls. Same call we had every week. Same routine. I didn't accuse anyone. I just asked what was happening with these deposits. The line went quiet. Then the call ended. No goodbye. No wrap-up. Just silence.

That scared me.

The next morning, I walked into the bank early, like always. I liked to check the place before opening. Make sure it was clean. Windows done. Trash out. I didn't get the chance.

A man was standing at my desk.

Tailored suit. Expensive. Furious. I didn't even sit down before he started in on me. He told me not to ask about money. Not to question accounts. Not to talk to anyone about deposits. He told me I was just a banker. To sit down. To shut up.

So, I did.

He explained, in his way, why it wasn't my business that the poor were gone and the powerful were swelling. I stood there with my arms at my sides. I wanted to cross them. I wanted to speak. I didn't.

Our weekly deposits used to hover around a million dollars. That was normal. Now they were twenty million. Thirty. Sometimes forty. And so much of it flowed straight to officials in town. No explanation. No paperwork.

At ten o'clock, the doors opened.

Two sheriffs came in. Loud. Bellowing. Calling my name across the lobby. I stepped out of my office. I wasn't going to hide. They took me right there.

I hadn't done anything. I had only asked a question.

They didn't let me use the bathroom. I had been running all morning. Coffee on an empty stomach. It hurt. They handcuffed me, locked my wrists to a bar in the van. I couldn't move. I couldn't hold it.

I let go.

I didn't care about their van. I needed the relief. I stayed soaked in that dress for days. Then weeks. Then longer.

They put me in a small cage with two other women. Barely room to lie down. We learned everything about each other. Every story. Every ache. Over two years, we watched one another shrink. Thin. Quiet. Fading. Dissolving.

That's how it happened.

That's how asking why turned into disappearing.

I can tell you how I survived, because I watched people die in those cages.

There were three of us women together. We were smarter than most, and we knew it from the first night. Fiona owned a sewing shop in the next town. She sold yarn to knitters. I loved her right away. I will never forget her. We are sisters now, for life. And Steph. Stephanie Rodriguez. She ran a landscaping business. Forty men on her payroll. Lawns, pools, Christmas lights. Whatever people needed. She had a sharp head for numbers and logistics. She will be my friend forever too.

The first night, sitting in my dress already stained, we made a decision. We were going to survive. Whatever that meant.

When food was thrown at us, we shared it. We didn't panic and eat it all at once like others did. We took care of each other. When guards came by and asked who could work, we all said yes.

Babies started coming in without their mothers. That broke us. Steph had the softest hands. She took care of the babies. Changed diapers. Held them when they cried. Fiona volunteered for administrative work. She told the guards she could help with records, files, numbers. She moved slowly into tracking who came in and who disappeared. I told them I could cook. I worked in the kitchen.

Nothing was free. Every privilege cost something. We gave pieces of ourselves every day just to stay alive and out of the cage.

One day, Fiona had a terrible toothache. We begged for medicine. Pain relief. Antibiotics. The guards said if we wanted help, we had to give something first. That was how it worked. We were slave labor in every sense of the word.

The worst part for me was the lack of cleanliness. One three-minute cold shower a week. That was it. I begged them to let us shut the water off halfway so we could soap and rinse. Same amount of water. They said no.

The air was sour. People cried constantly. The smell never left. I don't know how we made it, but we did. The sisterhood kept us alive.

When they finally said we were free, we didn't believe it. We thought it was a trick. The guards were gone before we even reached the doors. Within minutes, every one of them had fled. Keys were left behind. We opened cages. We carried children. We became mothers to hundreds of women in that place.

And then we walked out.

Now the government has given us money and temporary housing. I live among people who also survived, people who cannot go home. I will never return to my old job. I don't want it back.

What happened was wrong. Babies without mothers. Women in cages. Forced labor. We paid for anything with sex.

I will testify. I will stand in court and name names. I will make sure those responsible are held accountable for their actions. I hope they are raped repeatedly in jail.

I lost forty-five pounds I didn't have to lose. My shoes don't fit anymore. I came out wearing the same dress I went in with. Stained. Ruined. I'm keeping it. Sealed in a bag.

One day, if I have children or grandchildren, I will show it to them. I want them to see what survival looked like.

I didn't disappear quietly.

I fought to live.

I am glad it's over. I survived. But I don't know how much longer I could have lasted.

I will never be the same.

Chapter 3

ELEMENTARY SCHOOL TEACHER

NOT DETAINED BUT WANTED TO LEAVE A STATEMENT

New Jersey

I honestly don't know why teaching during that time was even needed. I think it was for the community. For us. So, I could go to work and look at the other teachers and say, can you believe this is what we're doing?

We were trying to keep the kids safe. Give them a meal. They weren't getting it anywhere else. They were scared. We had all those drills. You remember those. The saluting. The pledging. All the things they made us do.

Now we're free of that.

Now it feels worth being a teacher again.

Every class has kids with PTSD. One or two or three or four. So many came back skinny. One day a father dropped his son off and sat on the curb crying. I could see him through the window.

He didn't want to leave. We told him it was going to be okay. And it's. It really is.

I teach third grade. Third grade is supposed to be when kids can read and do math. But not my kids. We're starting over. Like kindergarten. We don't care about age or grade right now. School is about comfort. Joy. Safety.

We color a lot. We sit in circles. We talk. We don't worry about someone coming in to hurt them. We don't do those drills anymore. That alone changed everything.

The first year after it ended was strange. Everyone was relieved but still bracing. Like the fear was still sitting on your shoulder.

I remember throwing away my boots. I wore them every day in case I had to run with the kids. I didn't need them anymore. I threw them out.

Kids don't beg for their phones now. They just want hugs. They want to learn.

When our principal told us it was really over, we didn't know if we should tell the kids. We weren't sure it was real. He was a good man. We trusted him, but we'd been lied to so much.

I remember when they told us to take all the kids to the cafeteria. That day. I lost half my class. I'm still surprised they didn't take me.

I wore hoodies for a long time. Covered my hair. Then I bleached it blonde. We were all trying to disappear a little. We knew we couldn't take the kids home. We knew if we let them go at the end of the day, we might not see them again.

Now I hear kids laugh. Real laughing. We hadn't heard that in so long. We encourage laughter now.

We don't talk about the past much in class. We let kids talk if they need to. We listen. And we don't have to report it. That part still takes my breath away.

We watch shows about animals now. About saving the planet. We started a garden. Kids can leave class and go sit there if they want. One little kid just sat on a bench watching butterflies. Totally peaceful. We left him alone.

We took down some of the big walls around the school. That helped.

They say there's a pay raise coming. I believe it. They need us. We're not babysitters.

My husband says I don't know what to do with myself anymore. I'm happy to go to work, but I don't have that constant feeling of trying to save the kids every day. That takes getting used to.

The Pendulum Swings Back

I don't bring my gun to school anymore. That's not allowed now.

On Fridays, we have pajama day. We try to make things fun.

The cafeteria budget is bigger. Kids are eating. Filling out again. They'd been so thin. Tortillas. Broccoli. Fruit cups. That was it. Now they bring cupcakes and Ding Dongs. I don't care. Let them eat.

We're doing a musical. A talent show. Parents might come. We haven't had parents in the building in a long time.

One of the best things, honestly, was that there just wasn't any more talk about church. That whole thing stopped. It just stopped. When they took away the tax exemptions, that was it. That wasn't a bad thing.

We were fighting all the time before. Parents pulling kids out of school and putting them into those private religious schools. It was exhausting. When they shut that down and said there would be no religion without taxation, most of those places just disappeared. Except for the really big ones. That felt smart.

If something good came out of all of this, that might be it. We were pretending to believe things we didn't just so we wouldn't get in trouble. That still amazes me. I can't believe we lived like that.

We don't do the Pledge anymore. Thank God. No more of that. We just focus on getting kids back to being okay.

These little kids won't even know what cell phones are. I think that's brilliant.

No, I take that back. I don't want to say there was anything good about what we went through. Even before all this, parents were already hovering. Helicopter parents. They were part of the problem. Always demanding something. Grades. Exceptions. Complaints.

Now parents aren't allowed to interfere like that. I think that's smart.

Sometimes I think I might quit teaching. Now that I can see the kids are going to be okay. Maybe I'd rather make candles somewhere. Portland. San Francisco. Do something quiet. Something where I'm not responsible for holding together kids who are screaming inside.

We have so many counselors now. Maybe I should do that. Go back and get a counseling degree.

We know what matters now. It'sn't religion. That didn't save us. It caused more problems than it solved.

These kids have been through so much. I don't think being a third-grade teacher is enough to save them. They need real support. I'm doing what I can. We go outside a lot. We sit in the sun. Look at daisies. Watch bugs.

There's nothing wrong with that.

But when this year ends, and things feel lighter, happier, I might step away. I'd like to come back in a few years and see how they're doing. See if they made it.

The test scores are low. Some kids are confused by the alphabet. They don't know much yet.

But they need to learn.

So we don't do this again.

CHAPTER 4

NURSING HOME WORKER

Explaining The Purge

Utah

All of this sucks because now there are no old people.

That was my job. I liked my job. I took care of old folks. I worked in a center with about two hundred and fifty people. It wasn't enough staff, but I'm not complaining about that now. It feels like a lifetime ago. It feels like forever ago I had work.

They're going to have to figure out what to do with us. The workers. Because the old people are gone.

They weren't patients. I don't think that's the right word. They were people.

Nursing homes don't exist anymore. There's nobody old enough now to need them.

That part of the purge was scary.

One day the director came in and told us our jobs were over. Just like that. We asked if someone else was taking over. No. If someone new was coming in. No. If we were supposed to do anything. No.

We had schedules. Doctor appointments. Birthdays. A normal day. We were in shock. Nobody believed it.

There was a woman there, one of my favorites. She was an artist. I don't know why her family put her in a home. They just couldn't handle her. But she was lovely. She sang in her room. You'd hear her down the hall.

Some of the others kept the news on all day. It drained them. They got meaner. They wanted food. Diapers changed. They'd throw things if you brought the wrong thing.

We talked about unplugging the TVs. Taking phones away. Just to calm them. The families were calling and upsetting them. Everyone knew something was coming, but nobody wanted to believe it.

I heard from a friend who worked across town. She said they were wiping out nursing homes. I said no. That can't be right.

Then we were told to leave. Pack up. Go home. They said the residents would be taken care of. We didn't believe that.

I cried when I left.

I came back the next day.

The windows were broken. There was blood everywhere. No people. Just empty beds. Food half eaten. Diapers on the floor. Clothes. Shoes. Chairs turned over.

It was like everyone had vanished.

We knew it was possible. We had been warned. Other workers told us. Some stayed. I heard they disappeared, too.

None of our residents were under seventy. We were told they had lived full lives. That it was okay.

I don't know how they moved so many bodies so fast.

I found pictures on the floor. One woman with her family. She loved her grandkids. Loved when they brought the little dog.

Then visits stopped. Everyone was scared.

After that, I didn't have a job. I didn't have a purpose. I changed how I looked. Cut my hair. Wore old glasses. I didn't know what else to do.

I found my passport. It didn't matter anymore.

It was a numbers thing. Brown. Black. Didn't matter. Easy pickings.

Two hundred and fifty people. Gone.

That part is over.

The old people are gone.

And after a year, it's strange not having a whole generation anymore.

CHAPTER 5

ER DOCTOR
WHAT IT WAS LIKE
Chicago

The week before it all happened, I was thinking about killing myself.

Let me explain before you think I'm saying that just because I can look back now. It really was that bad. I couldn't believe this was where we were. I kept asking myself why I went to medical school. Why I wanted to be a doctor.

We were in the middle of an outbreak that never should have happened. It could have been prevented. But someone decided vaccines were the enemy, and the government went along with it.

We were looking at two-year-old children, thinking, " You shouldn't have this." We were looking at mothers and saying we didn't know if their child would live because they didn't vaccinate. We had children with polio. Polio. Coming in late, when it was already too far gone.

Wave after wave.

It wasn't just one thing. Everything was going backward. Diseases we knew how to stop were out of our control. We were practicing medicine like it was a hundred years ago.

Women came in carrying pregnancies that were not viable. You could see it on an ultrasound. Umbilical cords wrapped around necks. Missing skulls. Twisted bodies. I hate remembering it. I hate that it was only a year ago.

There was no hope. Not for the mother. Not for the child. Not for anyone.

I had a two-year-old who needed a heart. A new heart. We couldn't do it.

It made me not want to be a doctor anymore.

I'm ashamed of some of what I saw. Some of what I did. Some of what we were forced to do. It wasn't our fault. It was the government.

We had people walking the halls who weren't doctors. They had clipboards. Walkie-talkies. They reviewed charts and said things like, this isn't a viable person, stop treatment.

Just a few years earlier, we were fine. We had problems, sure. But we were doctors. We could act.

Then came the rules about pregnancy. We couldn't intervene. Mothers died. Fetuses died. We would stand there afterward, nurses and doctors, and just look at each other.

And then we'd come back the next day and do it again.

Before I thought about killing myself, I thought about leaving the country. Just packing a bag. Saying goodbye. Going somewhere that still practiced medicine.

Women became the scapegoat for everything. I saw pregnant children. Girls who should never have been in that situation.

One nurse's daughter came in in labor. Thirteen years old. The nurse didn't even realize her daughter was pregnant. She didn't want to see it. When we found out who the father was, it was exactly who you'd expect.

We weren't allowed to do anything.

Someone decided animal blood transfusions would work. For a while, we were giving dog's blood. I still don't understand how that was allowed.

There was no doctor in charge. Just chaos. Witchcraft. That's the only word for it.

They took away almost all antibiotics. Left us one. It barely existed. Vancomycin was impossible to get. Things that used to be minor became fatal.

A toothache. A dog bite. A scraped knee. An ant bite that turned into red streaks climbing up a woman's body. She died. We could have saved her before.

Surgery barely happened. Everything was triage. Gunshot wounds. Protest injuries. Bear spray in eyes. People bleeding out.

We were zombies. Doctors without authority. Without science. Without anyone steering.

When the end came, we ran into the streets like everyone else.

Suppliers who had been sitting on antibiotics showed up overnight. Shipping quantities. Pallets. Everything we had been begging for. Suddenly, we could do our jobs again.

It felt like we were doctors again.

We weren't suffering alongside the patients anymore. We could do the ordinary magic. Treat infections. Help a woman in distress. Do a C-section when it was needed. Let the mother decide. All the things that used to be normal.

It had been normal for so long. And then it became a death sentence if you misstepped.

The people judging us had no medical training. No degrees. But they had authority. If you did the wrong thing, you were done.

Now, we look at our new interns. They didn't finish medical school. School stopped when things got bad. That gap is real. We feel it.

The celebration wasn't just in the streets. It was in coffee shops. In cafeterias. In the ER. We were dancing. Crying. Laughing. Everyone was relieved in the same exhausted way. You could see it on our faces. We were near the end of ourselves.

It's going to take time to rebuild. People left. People were killed. People disappeared. People walked off and never came back.

Doctors went from respected to mocked. We were treated like a joke. Science was replaced by desperation.

I saw things I won't forget.

What surprises me is how fast some things came back once it was over. We don't really talk about it. That's strange. No one wants to live there. Everyone is forward-facing.

There are posters in the hospital now. *The good times are here again.* It feels like the Roaring Twenties. Dancing. Singing. Smoking. Drinking. Relief everywhere.

When I go home, though, the streets are quiet. Neighbors missing. Grocery stores were understaffed. Not enough people to grow food. Whole sections of life just… thinner.

I wanted you to know how hard it was for us. For everyone in medicine. Nurses. EMTs. Firefighters. Private practices that closed their doors and waited it out.

Now it's over.

I wish I could go back and tell people to hold on. The ones who didn't make it. Just stay a little longer.

All the restrictions on women are gone. Vaccines are back. We laugh now at the things they tried to replace medicine with. Bloodletting. Cod liver oil. It's grotesque.

It's only been a year. The memories come up. I laugh sometimes because it's over.

Before all this, we were curing things. Working with DNA. Making real progress. The world trusted us.

And then we lost so many people for no reason.

I still think about leaving. Mexico, maybe. Take my family. Start over. Be a country doctor somewhere small. Help people without all this weight.

I'm just relieved the end came.

I think everyone is.

Every minute of every day.

CHAPTER 6

RANCHER IN TEXAS
Vaccinating cattle

I don't know why you want to interview me. I don't really think I've got anything useful to say about this past year. I don't talk much. I don't really want to talk about before. I don't really want to talk about the end. I don't really want to talk about now either, except that it's better. It's better.

I will say this. Toward the end, our cattle weren't doing well. Whoever decided we weren't supposed to vaccinate animals anymore, that was just stupid. I fought that. I had medicine stashed away. Worming medicine. Everything you need to keep stock healthy. That's the job. You keep your cows healthy.

One morning about a year and a half ago, I came out to the ranch and I had no idea what was coming. Nobody was talking about it. It just happened. They showed up and said OKAY.

That's how I almost stopped being a rancher.

They took my cattle. No asking. No payment. They said it was for the good of the country. Said my cows were feeding soldiers on the front lines. You think soldiers needed filet mignon? Brisket? Hamburgers?

They took everything. I'd known those cows since they were born. I've been ranching my whole life in Texas. Then, suddenly, meat was coming from everywhere else, other countries. Then even that stopped.

Then they told us we couldn't sell our cows. Just keep them. We fought that. Hard. We weren't giving them up for free. What were we supposed to do?

I know what they were thinking. Free meat.

Except they didn't even use them. They didn't take them to slaughterhouses. They shot them. Pushed them into a gorge with a backhoe.

I'll never forget that sight.

They found out I'd vaccinated some of my cattle. That was enough. They wanted to make an example. Show the other ranchers what happens.

I don't know who told them. Maybe one of my hands. I had Mexican workers. Good workers. Hard workers. Those other boys would wander off, smoke, look at their phones. I'd have to tell them to get back to work. That made some people mad.

Someone talked. Someone always does.

I had to go home and tell my wife. We didn't have savings. We were already stretched thin. Suddenly, nobody was eating at our table.

Texas ranchers. Gone.

Texas is huge. We've had cattle here forever. Since before this country was even what it's. And suddenly, we were enemies because we kept our animals healthy.

It's been a year since things went back. That feels good. But it still stings. I don't have the capital to walk into a bank and say I want to start over. Cows are hard to get now. Real expensive.

Maybe chickens. I don't know. I don't like chickens. You have to watch them. Cows you can leave for a while and come back and see how they're doing. I've got fences for cows. Not chickens.

Everybody's figuring it out right now. That's what this year has been. Thinking. Being glad it's over. Thinking some more.

If I could do it again, I would've let that boy go. He was going to tell on me anyway. Those men without papers got caught eventually. Not on my ranch.

 That didn't come back on me. I was scared it would.

I did hide a couple of them.

They were good men.

CHAPTER 7

HISTORY PROFESSOR

PASSPORT VIOLATION

St. Louis

I seriously don't want to talk to you. I don't know why you've got a recorder. I don't know what you want me to say. You want me to say I'm happy? Happy that it's over? Why would I be happy?

Do you know how many times I was put into a detention camp? Just for being black. I've been black my whole life. My mother was black. Her father was black. All the way back. That didn't change because the government lost its mind.

I didn't do anything wrong. I taught history at a community college. Kids who didn't show up. Kids who couldn't stop looking at their phones. That was my crime.

The first time they took me, I was getting into my car. I'd gone to my office to grab a couple of books for the weekend. I didn't have my passport on me. Why would I? I'm an American citizen. I belong here.

That didn't matter.

They put me in a detention center. A month and a half later they let me out. No explanation. I think someone at the college said I was useful. One of the good ones. Even though I was never one of them.

They beat us. Kicked us. Tortured us. Made us eat off the floor. I broke a finger. I didn't fight back. They shaved my hair and laughed.

Instead of tattooing numbers like Auschwitz, they put our passport numbers on us. They said it was better that way. I asked why I needed a passport. They laughed and kicked me until I passed out.

My family didn't know where I was. I didn't know where they were.

When I got out and found my way home, I told everyone we weren't leaving the house. For six months, we barely did. Neighbors disappeared. We were threatened. Someone said they would make $1000 if they turned us in. I screamed, "We are Americans."

The second time, my whole family was grabbed. The camps were all very full. I didn't see my wife. I didn't see my kids. I just cried. They separated us.

Food wasn't served. It was thrown. We lived in cages. Survival of the fittest. It's hard still to even think about.

I don't want to remember it.

I don't want to believe it happened.

The day they let us out, I was skin and bones. My front tooth was gone and my head was shaved and yet lice lived on my head. I was filthy. I was wearing the same clothes for nine months. No toothbrush. No shoes.

When the doors opened, we didn't believe it. We thought it was a trick. We thought they'd slam them shut and laugh.

They had broken us. We didn't believe in God. We didn't believe in governments. We didn't believe in rescue.

I believed I might see my family again.

I was a history professor. I knew how this happens. I knew the steps. I knew the warning signs. I knew how long it takes when no one intervenes.

Why didn't anyone come? Why didn't any country evacuate us? Why did the world let this happen?

I learned the answer later.

When they let us out, we didn't know where we were. No food. No water. No shoes. No coats. Two or three hundred of us. Mostly black and brown. Some white. Some who didn't speak English. All regular people.

Government workers. Grocery clerks. Someone who posted the wrong thing online. There was a bounty on us. Turn someone in, get paid. At least that's what they said.

We walked down a dusty road. Someone found a stream. We drank from it. Got sick. Diarrhea. Lying on the side of the road.

They never told us why we were free.

Then we heard a town down the road.

Then we heard a town down the road. At least it sounded like a town.

There was hooping and hollering and clapping and crying and screaming. Cheering. Drum rolls. Pots and pans banging together. Everything at once. It scared us. We didn't know what it was. It sounded like a colosseum. Like people cheering while someone was being killed.

We didn't run. We were too tired. And there were people behind us pushing us forward anyway.

It took miles to get there. The town looked like something out of the 1800s. Dusty. Rusted. Turned over. And full of happy people.

They looked at us like, why are you here? They didn't know who we were. I don't know how every town didn't know there were camps just a few miles away, but they didn't.

They said, oh my God, it's over.

We said, what do you mean, it's over?

They told us. We still didn't really understand. We were just hungry. Thirsty. Barely clothed.

That town couldn't support us. There were too many of us. But they tried.

Someone turned on a hose. Not a shower, just a hose and old bar of soap. Would you strip naked in front of strangers just to feel clean? I did. But I only had my dirty rags to put back on.

An old woman came over and gave me a towel and an old pair of blue overalls. Said they were her husband's. I had no shirt. No underwear. No shoes. But the overalls were clean.

Someone opened a can of soup and handed it to me. No heat. No spoon. Just calories. Eat.

We wiped that town out. Food. Water. Kindness. Some people kept walking. They knew nothing would be left.

I laid down in the grass and slept. I don't know for how long. A day. Maybe more. People probably thought I was dead.

When I woke up, most people were gone. The town was quiet again.

Someone told me where I was. What date it was. What had happened. How to get home.

A school bus came. No tickets. No money. Just pick up and drop off. Every town along the way. People getting on. People getting off.

Eventually, I recognized where I was.

Someone gave me bread. Cheese. Half a Gatorade. I drank it like it was my salvation.

I was still wearing the old man's overalls. I was skin and bones. Missing a front tooth. But it was over.

When I got back to my apartment, everything looked the same. Just dusty. Quiet.

The neighbors had the key. They let me in. They fed me. I took a hot shower. Slept in my old bed. The one I shared with my wife.

I waited.

Weeks later, my wife and kids came back.

That was the reunion.

That's how I've spent this last year. Staying home. Healing. Trying to believe I'll never be caged again.

I'd rather be killed than caged.

I don't think it will happen again. I think we learned something.

One day, I'll have to teach this.

CHAPTER 8

UNATTRIBUTED STATEMENT
(recorded without identifiers, location withheld)

I don't want to talk to you.
I don't want my words carried around like proof or prayer or warning tape.
This was a bloody time. Say that much and stop.

I stayed off to the side. That's true.
Invisible is a skill. Silence is a skill.
People mistake that for innocence. It'sn't.

I won't count anything. Counting turns things into trophies.
I'm not here for trophies.

I will say this and only this: power does not collapse on its own.
It waits. It calcifies. It spreads its weight until the floor gives way.

People think history corrects itself.
It doesn't. It gets corrected.

I'm not interested in names.
Names make heroes and villains and erase

systems.
Systems are what matter.

Money moves faster than truth.
Fear moves faster than money.
Compliance moves faster than fear.

That's the order. Write it down.

I didn't invent anything.
I didn't lead anything.
I didn't save anything.

I stood inside a moment where many people decided the same thing at the same time for different reasons. That happens more than anyone wants to admit.

If you're relieved, don't trust that feeling.
Relief is a pause, not a cure.

If you're angry, good.
Anger means you're awake.
Just don't confuse it with permission.

This period being called "over" is administrative language.
It means the noise stopped.
It does not mean the machinery was dismantled.

You want a moral. I don't have one.
I have a warning, and even that is optional.

Nothing that happened required monsters.
Only ordinary people deciding that consequences were someone else's job.

That's all you get.
Don't look for me again.

CHAPTER 9

The Plumber
Texas

You want me to tell you what happened?

Alright. I'll tell you.

My family has been in Texas a long time. Long before all this mess. Generations. Yeah, my skin's brown. Yeah, I got a Mexican name. But my people came from Spain. I can trace it back. My mamá kept papers in a shoebox under her bed. She always said, *we belong here.* I believed her.

I had seven kids with three different women. Don't start with me. I worked. I paid bills. I showed up. I was a plumber. A good one. I made real money. Not rich money. But good money.

I voted for him. I did. I believed what he said.

My wife did hair and nails for rich ladies in town. She'd come home tired, hands hurting, telling me the things they said while she worked on them. Laughing. Joking. Talking ugly about folks like us. She'd smile and keep going.

That was her job. Me, I dealt with shit too. Literally. I'm a plumber. That's the joke.

But I mattered.

In my town, I was the plumber. Only one. Pipes broke, toilets flooded, somebody's kid flushed something dumb, they called me. I fixed things. I helped people. I worked next to them, ate lunch with them.

My mamá made tamales every Christmas. I sold them. Best damn tamales you ever had.

I was proud. Proud of where I came from. Proud to be American.

I never messed with a passport. That's what got me.

You don't need a passport to live in your own country. That's what I thought. My kids depended on me. Somehow, I went sideways and didn't even see it.

I think it was the news. That channel. The one that loved him. My mamá started watching it around 2014. All day. Every day. She loved him. Loved his wife. Said they talked plain. Said they told the truth.

That TV stayed on. All the time. I thought I was safe. Thought I was one of them.

I didn't know those old redneck boys had it out for me.

First time they messed with me, I thought it was nothing. A stop. A scare. They pulled me over. Hands on the hood. Cuffs on my wrists. Face in the dirt. Pulled me up. Then bam. Pistol to the face.

I kept saying, no, no, I'm one of you. I'm just like you. I just don't got my papers on me.

They said, you got papers?

I said I don't got a passport 'cause I'm American. I ain't going nowhere. You only need a passport if you're leaving. I'm not leaving.

I told them I was a plumber. Told one I fixed his roof leak. Told the other I saved him thirty grand on his septic. I knew their faces.

They just stared at me.

They kept me there over an hour. Threatened me. Finally said, get your paperwork straight. Get a passport. If you can't find it, go home to Mexico.

Mexico.

I went home shaking. Face all purple and swollen. My wife cried when she saw me. We looked into passports. Each kid cost money. Pictures. Birth papers. Fees. Too much. We didn't have it.

We told ourselves it wouldn't happen again.

I'd crossed borders before with my license. That was normal. Always had been.

After that, every time I drove through town, I felt eyes on me. I shut off the news. Told my kids to come straight home. You start warning them different. It ain't the scary man no more.

It's the scary man with a badge.

The night ICE came, they took me and my kids. Said we didn't have papers. Said they warned us.

They left my dogs. Left the birds. The fish. All my kids' animals. Blankets on the beds. Shoes by the door. School books on the table. Everything stayed.

I don't know where they took my family.

I know where they took me.

A cage near the border. The one my governor built. The one I voted for.

My mamá, same one glued to Fox News, finally called a lawyer. She had proof she was American. That made me American. That made my kids American.

Funny how that works.

Too late feels like a place you can't leave.

Seven months.

That's how long I was gone.

When I got back, the house was wrecked. Plates smashed. Cabinets dumped. Drawers pulled out like somebody went looking for a secret that wasn't there. Water off. Power off. Yard dead. Dogs gone. Why even come back at all.

The house was already in foreclosure. Didn't even sting. Felt right, somehow. Like the place knew it wasn't ours anymore.

My neighbor came over. The one with all the flags. Five of them. Been flying there forever. Only swaps them out when they rot. All saying the same thing. Same thing I used to believe.

He laughed when he saw me.

Well hell, looks like they took you, ha ha. Looks like they ruined your life, ha ha.

Guess they didn't know you were such a good guy, ha ha.

Everything was funny to him. That kind of laugh people do when they don't wanna feel bad. Nothing was funny to me. I lost my house. Lost my tools. Probably lost every customer I ever had. Didn't even know where my wife was yet.

That laughing made me sick.

I thought I was one of them. Turns out I never was. I think they knew it the whole time.

I did everything right. Gave discounts. Smiled. Fed their dogs when they went on vacation. Showed up in the middle of supper when something busted and they needed it fixed *right now*.

None of it mattered.

Why stay in the house. There wasn't nothing left. Maybe a fork in a drawer. No plates. No lights. No water. No phone. No TV.

I didn't know what to do.

I'd just spent seven months in a cage. Sleeping on concrete next to men I didn't know. Treated worse than dogs. I don't even speak Spanish. My mamá does. I understand some. I wasn't one of them either. And I didn't have the papers they wanted.

Back then we didn't know it would take years to fix any of this.

They say the last year been a relief for most folks. Before that, I waited in that house. No power. No water. Just waiting. Waiting for my wife. Waiting for my kids.

When they finally came back, it was just crying. All of it crying. Little kids. They'd been caged. I don't know what they went through. They couldn't talk about it. Too broken.

My wife and kids were separated. Five girls. Two boys. I don't know where they were or what they saw.

I didn't know what to do.

Passports felt impossible. I knew it was over the first time they pulled me over. Knew it in my bones. I was gonna lose everything.

I went to the bank and pulled out what cash I could. When they talked foreclosure, I didn't care. Take it. Bad memory anyway.

I bought an RV trailer. Old. Cheap. Traded equipment for it. Stuff I worked years to own. At least we had wheels.

I didn't invite my mamá. Even though she got me out. I still blame her. If that TV hadn't been on all day cheering for that man, the liar, the cheat, maybe none of this would've happened.

I told my kids to grab their school books. Nothing else. We went back one last time for food. Paper plates. Whatever we could use. Had to leave before anyone noticed.

We drove.

West Texas. Empty land. Filled water where we could. Used the bathroom outside. Hid the trailer under trees. Scavenged food. Lived like rats.

Outside Laredo, ICE got us again.

Handcuffs. Vans. Yelling.

They separated us. My wife screaming. I don't know where my kids went.

The men's camp was worse. Hotter. Time didn't mean nothing. I didn't know where my family was.

They beat us. Starved us. Kicked us.

For what.

No passports.

That's all they ever said.

They threw oatmeal on the floor.
No passport. Here you go.

I told them I needed money to get passports. They didn't care.

They were crazy men. Doing it for fun. Terrorizing people because they could.

Then one day they opened the door and said, you're free.

Free.

No reason. No explanation. Some men stayed in the cages. Thought it was a trick.

I watched the uniforms leave. Cars gone. All of them.

It was just us.

My wife and I had a plan. If we ever got separated, we had a way to find each other. Something to hold onto.

I rode a train. Other folks did too. People saying it was over. Saying things would go back to normal.

Hard to believe.

I lost everything.

I walked back to the house. Broken windows. Empty rooms.

I made a cot in one of my kids' rooms. Put a little white flag on the door. Told my wife if she saw it, I was there. If not, keep going.

I been waiting a year now.

She hasn't come back. My kids haven't come back.

People say the end is here. People are smiling. People are happy.

For me, it never ended.

I don't know what to do.

I planted a garden. I hunt squirrels and deer. I fish. I work at night so nobody sees me. I keep the windows blocked.

I don't trust it. I still think they'll come back.

They say help is coming. Money. Aid. A fresh start.

But if my family ain't here, what's that mean.

So I stay.

The Pendulum Swings Back

I live like an animal.

I'm not happy it's over. I'm not happy he's dead, even though he caused all this.

I voted for him.

I was part of it.

Until I wasn't.

CHAPTER 10

Military Man
No NAME GIVEN
No location allowed

Taking down a billionaire, yeah. That was almost kind of fun. Don't mention my name in this story or where you found me or how you came about my name. I am not part of that group. I'm not on social media. I don't have a website. I don't have a family or a mother. You can't trace me.

But if you do, you will be sorry.

But I will tell you a few things. Not because I'm proud of it, but because the world should know some things that are true.

Now, how it all worked, that again can't be told. Not gonna be told. What it was that we did, that isn't gonna be told either.

If AI gets unfolded one day, that'll be fine, but I don't want my name associated with it. And it did take a lot of people to make it happen, to make it all work. There's only so many billionaires in the world, so it's easy to figure out which of the top 10 should we target.

It's only gonna help the world. It's like taking out a monster or 10 monsters.

We'll let everything else fall in place once we've done the hard work. It's kind of like the movies you see on Netflix.

A lot of behind the work, a lot of people, a lot of people that had to still their guts and take one for the team, even.

Some of the closest people to these billionaires secretly hated them, hated them because they had been up close and seen how evil they actually were and how they just stepped on people to become billionaires.

They didn't work hard for this money, but they caused a lot of damage. You know, the kind that don't pay their contractors, don't pay for the building, don't pay for this.

They say they're gonna pay for it, and then smoke and mirrors. I hate those people, too. It wasn't that hard. Finding them, that took the inside, skinny. So, there's money involved.

There's secrets that have to be kept. There's blackmail involved. It all belongs to somebody, all that information, and we didn't just get it out of the ether.

We were told things. We were given information, locations, rendezvous points, who was gonna be there, what the security was like, what kind of ammunition and guns were they carrying.

It all came to us in bits and pieces. Some spycraft. We did have some toys involved. It wasn't hard, but it wasn't easy.

But it was needed to reset the world order and the economy back to a little bit more even. Because these bastards, they didn't pay taxes.

They weren't fair. They didn't want to give one penny to anybody who they didn't absolutely have to pay, else those people would turn against them. And they knew the gig. There was a couple of them that I was pretty dang proud to get rid of. You can guess who those are. And because there were some really big people at the top of this that got us involved and made it worth our while, those people, they never will be found out. You're probably looking at them right now on the TV.

There's no accountability for these people. They are the authority and they authorized it. Compliance was normal and we were just helping out.

So, you're happy, you're joyful. Yay! Yay! The billionaires are dead. The other billionaires that didn't die are scared. They're old, so they'll die soon. We'll make sure of it. We'll also make sure that there's no wills in place that keep it from going to another family member. Those documents are all burned.

This money goes back to the people. It goes back into the coffers to pay for Social Security, to pay for Medicare and Medicaid and school lunches and kids that need glasses and kids that need help in school. Like, I can't believe we let this go on for so long. It's like a little picnic.

We're all gonna go on a little picnic and open up our little sandwiches and our little fruit baskets and our little bottles of wine. And we're just gonna sit there and enjoy it for a while, just savor the fact that we've got to this point right now.

We didn't have to burn down houses or blow up bridges or sink a few yachts. Didn't take that.

Just this and that and this and that. You could fill in the blanks. You know how it all happened, so I'm not gonna give you any details, except to say, do you really feel like I should be judged for this? I don't wanna be a hero, but I'm not going to jail for this because I helped millions and millions of people. And the government better suck it up.

They got what they wanted. They got money back into the coffers.

Money that they had been spending on I.C.E. and for every little doodad and this doodad and all kinds of different equipment that we did not need to hunt down American citizens.

We didn't need to spend that money. Good grief. That's probably the worst of it, the time lost. Can you imagine if that jerk hadn't gotten in to become a president, if things would have worked out like they should have, until some billionaire got involved and another billionaire got involved and another billionaire got involved and they got it all wackadoo. Ruined our elections.

Started having people disappear. Oh, what a mess. Really, they deserve what all they get. And if I could teach you how to do what I did, so that we could get rid of all of them, that would be my assignment. Not to be just removed, but to be finished. And all those billionaires, get down to what? How many billionaires do we need, really? None. Or a trillionaire?

Yeah, we don't need that either. And we don't need to go to Mars, and we don't need to do this, and we don't need to do that.

Like, let's just save the planet. That's my whole thing.

If I could save some little baboon on the other side of the world, some little monkey somewhere that needs to be saved, I'd save some shit.

CHAPTER 11

Eleven-Year-Old Boy

Birmingham, Mississippi

I really don't really know how to talk good about it. I'm only eleven. I wasn't old enough to understand grown-up things yet. But I remember nights they took us. I remember the yelling and the screaming and the trucks and the lights. I remember the dogs barking like they knew something bad was happening too.

They put me with a bunch of kids. Some younger than me. Some older. No school. No mom. No dad. Just yelling and shouting and too many bodies in a row. Some kids cried. Some didn't even know how to cry anymore.

I remember the smell. Not like home. Not like cookies or dirt after rain. A smell that sticks in your nose like a bruise. I remember thinking if I never smelled that again I'd be happy.

I tried to think about my birthday once. I couldn't.
I couldn't think about nothing good.
Only about being free.

When they opened the gate, I was too scared to move. I thought it was another trick. Maybe they were gonna lock us back up again. That's what my heart kept saying.

But we walked outside. It was loud. Too loud. Too bright. Too free. My legs felt funny. Like they forgot how to work.

I still don't like loud noises.
I still don't like big places.

I still wake up at night thinking someone's coming to take me again.

People say it's over.

It don't feel over to me.

But I'm trying.

CHAPTER 12

THE INFLUENCER
SOCIAL MEDIA CRIMES
Louisianna

Let me start at the beginning.
Because it really started way before everything fell apart.

I just wanted to be an influencer. I don't even know how long that idea had been sitting in my head. Instagram, TikTok, whatever platform came next. I watched so many people make it look easy. Like, do this, post that, get followers, and then the followers turn into money and suddenly you don't need a real job anymore.

It felt possible. It felt easy. And honestly, I liked doing it.

I remember when he first came down that escalator. I was on Twitter back then. I was on Twitter every single day. Yelling at my phone. Literally screaming at the screen. Just furious at how ugly it all was from the very beginning.

Do you remember how ugly it was? I don't even know what the worst part of that first term was anymore. Was it the McDonald's hamburgers for the athletes at the White House? Or was it COVID? Or was it something new every single day?

Every night my husband and I sat on the couch watching the news, feeling completely helpless. Every fucking night.

Then I'd go back to Twitter and scream some more.

Eventually, they shut my account down. I don't even remember exactly what did it. Something about Humpty Dumpty falling off the wall and not being able to be put back together again. It tied into something in the news at the time. It felt harmless. It felt stupid. But I had a lot of followers. Like, a hundred thousand followers.

And they shut me down.

After that, I moved to Instagram, but not right away. I let it cool off. I told myself I was done. And honestly, it felt good. It felt like relief. Like I wasn't carrying around all that anger anymore.

My job got busy. Life got busy.

Then things got bad again. He got elected again.

At first, I wasn't even creating content. I was just reposting. Remixing. Whatever they call it. I wasn't hunting for stories. I wasn't making anything up. I wasn't pushing conspiracy stuff. I was just doing what everyone else was doing.

I did vote Democrat. They knew that. Voter rolls exist.

My Instagram kept growing. Eighty thousand followers. And I still wasn't saying anything extreme. No threats. No calls to violence. No conspiracy theories. I wasn't even trying to make money from it. I had a job. Social media was just how I blew off steam.

And yeah, it became a little obsessive. I checked it every day. Needed the fix. That dopamine hit. They say it's addictive. I guess I was addicted.

My husband and I talked a lot about the rumors. About what might happen if things went bad. We'd seen other accounts disappear. Go dark. We knew why.

We had a go-bag. Cash. Some disguises. Cars that could go far. A generator. Supplies. We talked through scenarios. I'm a planner. I was a Girl Scout. I like plans.

If we had to bug out, I knew what I'd grab.

My husband had weapons. We had a second place, a weekend place we thought we could go to if needed.

Then people started getting killed. And we knew that was the trigger.

And then the trigger happened.

After that, everything unraveled fast.

There was no knock on the door. It was just a crash. They were inside. Total chaos. No time to grab anything. No time to put on real shoes. I didn't even have a bra on. I was working from home. Casual clothes. My husband had just gotten home from work.

We heard they were in town. We didn't know they were in our neighborhood. It still felt far away. Like it wouldn't happen to us.

I'm white. My husband's family came over on the Mayflower. We had passports. I just couldn't get to them. Not with all that noise and yelling and confusion.

They had a dog. Barking. Sniffing. I think it was to see if we were hiding anyone. We weren't.

They didn't give us time to explain anything.

They grabbed my laptop. Grabbed me. Hands behind my back. Handcuffs. Blindfold. Same with my husband. They took his keys. Took the truck.

They separated us immediately. Different vans. He went one way. I went another.

That was terrifying.

After that, I lost track of time. Days blurred together. I couldn't tell you how long anything lasted.

They put me in a place that was freezing cold. Concrete floor. No sweater. No blanket. No pillow. Just here you are. This is your life now.

There were ten of us women in that room. Short women. Tall women. Different ages. Different backgrounds. We all just stared at each other in shock.

The men might have handled it differently, I don't know. But for us, the cold was unbearable. At night we huddled together on the floor just to share body heat. Just to feel another human being.

I don't know how long that went on. I lost a lot of weight. They barely fed us. Sometimes a cup of water. Sometimes nothing.

If you wanted food, you had to do things.

I'm not going to talk about that part. That's not what you're asking, and I don't want to say it out loud.

By the time I was in that prison, the system had decided I was a bad person.
And I wasn't. I wasn't doing anything different than what millions of people were doing online every day.

That's what social media is. It keeps us engaged so we make content so someone way up there, billionaire row, makes money off all of us. That's the system. I was just part of it. A cog. A tiny little cog. Not important. Not powerful.

I don't even know how long I was in that detention center. I'd have to sit there later and look at dates and think, they took me here, then I was here, then I was back here again. Time didn't make sense anymore.

The truth is, they let my husband go before me.

That was the hard part.

When he finally made it back to our house, he had to walk a long way. They had detention centers everywhere by then. Kind of local ones. So he was close enough to walk home.

But when he got there, someone else was living in our house.

Just like that.

He said it was like his brain couldn't catch up. He didn't know what to do because he knew I would be coming back too. So he stayed nearby. Slept in an unlocked car at night. Watched the house. Just in case I showed up.

He waited for weeks like that.

Then the miracle happened. Like a real miracle. The kind you don't even let yourself imagine because you're already so far down the well you're just trying to breathe.

I remember when they came to get me, thinking, what should I grab? Should I grab soap? Because I knew I'd be dirty. I knew I'd want to wash. I didn't have time. I didn't even have time to grab my phone.

It was ugly. It was fast.

And then when the end came, it was just as fast.

Everything shifted. All at once. The air changed. Things moved from far right back toward the middle. Toward something that felt human again. And suddenly the doors were open.

They let me out. Prison. Detention. Whatever you want to call it.

I could barely walk. I'd make it maybe a quarter mile, then I'd have to sit down. Then another quarter mile. Then sit again. I was starving. I was so thirsty.

There were fewer people on the streets. Fewer cars. But somehow, there were people celebrating. From a distance. You could feel it. Like the atmosphere had changed.

All I wanted to do was get home.

Someone stopped and asked if I wanted a ride.

I didn't trust them. Not at all. I was terrified of being taken again. I watched their face. I listened to their voice. I talked to them before I got in the car. I didn't say my street name. I didn't say exactly where I lived. I still thought it might be a trick.

I hadn't seen a newspaper. I hadn't seen a phone. I hadn't seen a date. I didn't know if any of this was real.

I looked like I was about to fall into a grave. A walking skeleton. No sun. No food. Same clothes. By then, I was wearing donated scrubs. I hadn't seen myself in a mirror in years.

Some of the people who helped me feel... unreal now. Like they were angels or something. I don't remember their faces clearly. I don't remember the car. I just remember the feeling of being guided forward.

Just keep going. Keep going.

And I made it back.

My husband saw me and ran to me. And we just stood there holding each other, saying the same thing over and over.

I can't believe that happened.
I can't believe we survived.
I can't believe we're alive.

It was the worst thing either of us has ever lived through.

There won't be movies about this. They shut that down fast. A year of settling. No social media.

Low-tech phones only. Honestly, it was probably necessary. Everyone needed to decompress. Our bodies needed it.

We were starving. We just needed to eat.

Then the money started coming. Aid. Help. Repatriation funds. They removed the people who were illegally living in our house. We cleaned it. Fixed it. Made it ours again.

It feels... mostly right.

But at night, we don't watch the news. We don't watch anything. We sit together. Sometimes we do puzzles. Sometimes we play cards. We hold each other. We're making up for lost time.

I'll never go back to social media. Even if it comes back. It did too much damage. To families. To the country.

I blame the media. All of it. When I look at it now, that's what I see. The system broke us.

If the people in charge say we need a pause while they rebuild something more balanced, I'm okay with that.

We gave our cabin in the woods to a family who had nothing. We might go north. Canada, maybe. Start over. Be safe.

I feel broken. I don't want opinions anymore. I don't want to fight. That part of me is gone. I just want a place to live and enough to survive.

Did I bring this on my husband? Maybe not. They had voter rolls. They knew exactly how both of us voted.

Paper ballots now. Fine by me.

It was the worst time of our lives. But it's behind us. The next years will be better.

There are fewer of us now.

Everything feels different.

Is that what you wanted to know?
What it felt like to survive?
What it feels like now?

It's still shocking.

It still feels painfully real.

CHAPTER 13

Teenage Girl

Arizona

So yeah. You wanna know what it was like back then. And what it's like now.

I just turned eighteen. That matters. Because everything that happened to me happened before I was grown. I was fourteen when they took me. Seventeen when they let me out. So yeah. I guess I grew up in a cage. That's not dramatic. That's just the math.

The night it happened wasn't special. That's the part people never get.

It wasn't a protest.
It wasn't a raid.
It wasn't loud or planned or anything like that.

We were coming home from a basketball game.

We won. We were hyped. All girls. All friends. One of the dads driving, dropping everyone off. We were loud, talking over each other, replaying the game, singing with the radio even though nobody knew the words right.

It felt safe.
It felt normal.
It felt like being fourteen.

Then we hit traffic.

Just dumb stuff. Somebody forgot their bag. Someone else took too long leaving the gym. A light backed up. Normal life.

And just like that, we were fifteen minutes past curfew.

We saw the lights before we understood what was happening. Police cars ahead. Lanes blocked. Someone waving us over like it was nothing. Like routine.

The dad said stay calm. Said it was fine. Said it was just curfew.

Then they told us to get out of the car.

We started crying. Screaming. Begging. We'd been taught our whole lives not to get out of the car. Ever. But they didn't ask. They yanked us out. Fast. Rough. Like we weren't girls. Like we weren't kids.

Hands behind our backs. Cuffs on. All of us lined up on the side of the road.

For curfew.

I remember thinking, this can't be real. Someone's gonna stop this. Someone's gonna say this is too much.

Nobody did.

They put us in vans. Didn't tell us where we were going. Didn't let us call our parents. Didn't let us grab anything. Clothes. Phones. Nothing.

We just vanished.

That's how it started.

The camp was dirt floors and cots. No pillows. No blankets at first. Too many people everywhere. Bugs. Lice. Always noise. Always someone crying.

We were fourteen. Fifteen. Some younger.

They told us if we wanted things, we could get them. A cigarette. A candy bar. Extra time outside. Quiet. Favors.

You just had to use your body.

That's how they said it.

I didn't. I'm not saying that to sound brave. I'm just saying it because it's true. But I watched other girls do it. And I don't judge them. Not for one second. When you're hungry and scared and someone dangles something small in front of you, your brain stops working right.

Time didn't make sense in there. Days smeared together. Months disappeared. We didn't see the sky much. Seasons didn't exist. I stopped caring about my birthday. School. The future.

When they let us out, I was seventeen.

No warning. No reason. One day the doors opened and they said go.

Some girls didn't believe it. Thought it was a trick. I almost stayed. That's how scared I was.

But it was real.

I came out skinny. Quiet. Older than I should've been. Everything felt too loud. Too open. Like the world might snap shut again if I moved wrong.

Now, I'm eighteen.

People say it's over. And yeah. The big thing ended. Everybody knows that. But just because something's over doesn't mean it's gone.

I still freeze when I see police lights.
I still check the clock without thinking.
Sirens still mess with my stomach.

I'm trying. There are groups now. PTSD stuff. Support groups. People who get it.

I'm still angry. Because we did nothing wrong. We were American kids. Girls coming home from a basketball game.

If anyone ever asks me to testify, I will. No hesitation. I'll say everything.

For now, that's all I got.

CHAPTER 14

Switch Technician
California

I wasn't important. That's the first thing you need to understand.

I didn't work for the government. I didn't wear a uniform. I didn't make policy. I worked nights at a regional data facility outside the city. Climate-controlled floors, humming racks, red and green lights blinking like they always had.

My job was uptime.

I had a badge. A checklist. A supervisor who never raised his voice.

When the first directive came down, it wasn't dramatic. It was a maintenance notice. Temporary throttling. Regional segmentation. National security language, all very clean and boring. I signed off on it like I signed off on everything else.

You don't think about faces when you're staring at a terminal.

Then it escalated.

We were told certain routes would be darkened. Certain redundancies removed. Certain systems "paused." The word pause did a lot of work back then.

I remember asking, just once, what would happen to emergency traffic.

My supervisor said, "It's being handled elsewhere."

That's the phrase that let everyone sleep.

I never saw anyone get arrested. I never heard screams. I never saw a cage. I drove home, ate leftovers, watched old shows on a hard drive because streaming got spotty.

At work, the lights kept blinking.

The day they brought in the government liaison, he didn't look scary. He wore a blazer that didn't fit right and drank vending machine coffee. He thanked us. Said we were patriots. Said history would remember infrastructure workers kindly.

That was the first time I felt sick.

Because I realized something then. Not all at once, but enough.

Nothing happens without systems.

Not silence. Not isolation. Not disappearance.

Those require cooperation.

One night, I was told to pull a redundancy manually. No automation. Hands-on. I hesitated. Just for a second.

My supervisor said, "If you don't, someone else will."

So I did.

I went home and couldn't sleep. I kept thinking about how quiet my phone felt. How small the world had gotten without me noticing.

When it ended, nobody came for us. No hearings. No apologies. No trials.

They just told us to restore.

Flip it back on.

Bring the routes online.

Reconnect the world.

We did it in under six hours. Faster than any drill we'd ever run.

People danced in the streets.

The Pendulum Swings Back

I sat at my terminal and watched the traffic surge and thought,
It turns out the hardest part wasn't turning it off.

It was knowing how easy it had been.

CHAPTER 15

The Studder
(He wanted to be recorded
Utah

I heard
I heard
I heard you were looking

I heard that you were looking
sorry about my stutter
it comes and goes
like the truth

I heard you were looking for people to talk to
to talk to
about what we saw

I'm not gonna say what we saw

I'm gonna say what I didn't see

I didn't see a plaque

I didn't see a plaque where thirty-two people
were gunned down
by you-know-who

You know who
you know who they were

There's no names
no names
no names at all

No sign of the blood
no shadow where it soaked in
no marker

No marker
none

Maybe it was in the paper
maybe
once
and that was it

None of those people mattered enough
none of them mattered at all

They were just shot
and their bodies taken
who knows where

Who knows where
I don't know where

There's no acknowledgement now that it's "over"
no roll call

The Pendulum Swings Back

no list
no wall

No talk about the disappeared
about the cases still open

Crack on my mother's back
crack-a-doodle
crack it open

Crack if you're Black
crack if you're Hispanic
crack
crack
crack

I want some crack
that's who I am
the crack master

I just can't remember where my crack is

But I don't see plaques
where there should be plaques
all over the U.S.

In some places
you know where they are

In some places, they're hidden
hidden so good
they'll never be found

Until someday
when they build a big suburb
you know
a big suburb

Suburb
sorry about my speech impediment

And someday those bones will come back up
they always do

And we'll have to ask
whose body is this
what body is that

How many bodies are there

Why do they all have bullet holes in their heads

What happened here

What happened here

Why aren't we talking about this

Yeah
it might be "over"

But there are still bodies
in the closet
on the side of the road
in shallow dirt

The Pendulum Swings Back

You can't bring that back

You can't unbury it

CHAPTER 16

Mail Carrier
Washington State

I didn't think it would be me. That's the truth.

I was just the mailman. Same route for twelve years. Same dogs. Same old ladies waiting by the window. Same busted mailboxes I fixed with duct tape because nobody else would.

You learn a lot delivering mail. You know who's sick. Who's lonely. Who's getting evicted. Who's waiting on a check that didn't come yet. You don't open envelopes, but you don't have to. You feel it in the weight of the paper.

When things started changing, my job didn't.

At first.

They told us we were essential. That word meant something then. We got badges. Letters we could show if we were stopped. "Federal service," it said. I kept it folded in my wallet like a prayer.

Then the mail started getting lighter.

No magazines. No catalogs. No birthday cards. Fewer letters. A lot of official-looking envelopes with no return address.

People stopped waving.

Some houses stopped answering the door at all. Mailboxes filled up. I was told to keep delivering anyway. "Don't hold," the memo said. "Don't mark vacant unless confirmed."

Confirmed by who, I never knew.

One day, I noticed something strange. Same house. Same name on the box. But the mail kept changing. Different government logos. Different fonts. All heavy paper. All serious.

I knocked once. Just once.

Nobody answered.

The next week, the box was gone.

Just gone.

After that, I stopped knocking.

I kept my head down. I delivered what I was told. I told myself it wasn't my job to ask questions. I told myself someone else knew more than I did. I told myself I needed the paycheck.

I had a wife. Two kids. Mortgage.

Then came the reroutes.

We were told certain addresses were no longer active. Skip them. Don't mark anything. Just skip. Like they'd never been there.

That was when it hit me.

Mail isn't just paper. It's proof. It's a connection. It's how you know you exist in the system. When you stop getting mail, you disappear quietly.

I watched whole streets go silent without a sound.

The day it ended, nobody told us ahead of time. The scanners just updated. Routes restored. Addresses reactivated.

I delivered letters to houses that hadn't seen paper in years.

Some doors opened. Some didn't.

One woman cried when she saw a stack of envelopes with her name on them. She kept touching them like they might vanish again.

I didn't say anything. I just handed them over.

I still deliver mail.

But I keep thinking about how close I was to being the last person to see someone's name before it vanished.

And how easy it was to keep walking.

CHAPTER 17

Imprisoned for Rioting
Portland, Maine

I can talk about how it ended for me, but I need to say this first. They used a long-range acoustic device on us, and I have severe tinnitus now. I lost most of the hearing in my ears. That is the price I paid. I suppose I am lucky they did not do worse.

Even after the chemical sprays, the smoke, the bear spray, I kept going out. I went every day. This was my country. I believed standing there mattered. People always talk about the American Revolution like it was clean and noble. It was not. I told myself this was no different. You pay something when you stand up.

When they finally took us, my family had no idea where I was. They assumed I had disappeared like so many others. I am an American citizen. I had done nothing illegal. I was not armed. I was not threatening anyone. I was on the ground when the device went off, bleeding from my ears, unable to stand. That is when they picked us up.

They handcuffed us and loaded us in. It was uglier than I expected. They wore masks. You could only see their eyes. I could not look at them. I should have had protection for my ears, but no one warned us. That part was a surprise.

We were interrogated for days. They kept us awake. Our ears were still bleeding. No one treated us. No one listened. There were about forty of us. They put us in cages, ten to a cage, men and women together. There was a bucket for a toilet. No paper. That was the worst part. The humiliation.

The first day they gave us nothing. No food. No water. We sat there looking at each other, trying to understand how this was happening. We knew our history. Kent State. Martin Luther King. We knew what this country had done before. Still, when it's happening to you, it feels impossible. There was too much at stake to walk away. That is what I told myself.

A couple of years later, it ended. They released us. But there was no return to a normal life. My family thought I was dead. They sold my car. My phone was gone. I did not know any numbers by heart anymore. It was like being born again, except I could not hear.

We were put out on the street. Everyone was celebrating. Yes, people were happy. But we had no money. We could not even take a bus. We stood on the side of the freeway asking strangers for help. One trucker picked us up. He was crying and angry. We got out as fast as we could. Not everyone was relieved. Not everyone was safe.

Most of us were from the same small town in Iowa. The first thing we did was find a newspaper. Two years had passed. We were trying to understand what had happened while we were gone. Hungry, exhausted, wearing the same clothes, we looked like ghosts.

There were still people looking for revenge. You could feel it. Millions had come out of the camps. Millions standing there asking what came next. There was no plan waiting for us.

Eventually, I made it home. I knocked on my parents' door. They were crying before I even stepped inside. It was hard to explain what I had been through. Harder still to hear their questions. Losing my hearing was hard for them to accept. I told them I was alive. That had to be enough.

I am glad it's over. I am. But it will always be on my record. They did not erase that. Maybe they should have. Some money is coming now to help us start again.

Before all of this, I was an electrician. I had a good job. I was trying to build a life. Now people look at me differently. They ask what kind of protester I was. You have to explain yourself over and over.

I tell them the truth. I was not one of the bad ones. I was just there.

I got caught up in social media because I wanted to matter. I did not want to look back someday and say I sat on the sidelines and watched it happen. They had the voter rolls. They knew who we were. They were watching us long before we knew it.

They tracked our cars. They listened to our calls. They read our posts. WhatsApp, messages, everything. We were new to this. We were not professional protesters. We did not understand the level of surveillance. They had already built the case. We were just waiting for the moment they decided to act. Chickens in a coop. Fish in a barrel.

The nights inside were the worst. I hope I stay in touch with the people I was imprisoned with, though they separated men from women, so it's mostly the men I still think about. For two years we planned. We imagined what we would do if we got out and the world was still broken. We made up secret languages. We talked in fragments when we could. Hunger makes the mind sharp in strange ways. We thought about revenge. We thought about justice. We thought about making things right.

We never got the chance.

One day they opened the doors. The lights went off. They walked out. No explanation. No warning. Nothing. At first we thought it was a trap. We had seen too much to trust anything. But they did not come back.

Now that I am home, I live with PTSD. I don't go out at night. I don't watch television unless there are captions. That part works well enough. I am relieved it's over. I am glad I stood up. I paid a price, but not as high as some.

I think I will work again as an electrician. The doctors say they might be able to help my hearing. What they used on us should have been outlawed. That acoustic device damaged people permanently. I want to understand how it was used and why. I want that knowledge to be there for others someday, if they ever face something like this again.

I live with my parents now. We use a whiteboard. We have our own kind of sign language. Losing your hearing is one of the hardest losses. You go into a room and the world turns into muffled sounds. You cannot join in. It's isolating.

The same is true for the others who were with me. Forty people at that protest. All of us changed. In prison we wrote messages in the dust because we had no paper or pencils. That's how we held on.

I am telling this so it's known we were not bad people. We were standing up for our town. For our lives. For what we believed in. I am not threatening anyone now. But I need acknowledgment. Harm was done.

Things are calmer now. Faces on the street look lighter. People are not afraid. It's astonishing how fast the world can change when one thing finally breaks.

We are back in the light. I hope it lasts. If I ever have children, I hope they never have to live through anything like this.

That is my story.

CHAPTER 18

Alabama Preacher

Imprisoned for Domestic Terrorism

I'm a preacher from Alabama.
My daddy was a preacher.
My granddaddy was a Baptist minister.

I come from a long line of men who stood behind pulpits and spoke like they knew the truth of things. I used to be one of those men. I'm not anymore.

What happened to me didn't happen all at once. That's the hardest part to explain. It came slow. Quiet. So quiet I didn't even know it was happening until it already had.

At first, we were part of the group. We were told what to say and what not to say. It was framed as guidance. As protection. As keeping the peace.

We didn't have many Black or brown folks in our congregation, but my congregation knew them well enough. Lived near them. Worked near them. Saw them every day. And still, they carried hate in their hearts.

Every Sunday, I preached love, peace and kindness. I preached about feeding people, teaching folks how to survive, standing up for children, standing against men who hurt the vulnerable. I tried to show them another way. A way that didn't end with people being taken in the night.

We were a small community. Everybody knew everybody, or at least thought they did. I'd go to the hospital in the next town when folks were dying. I'd sit by their beds, hold their hands, pray with them. I did it even when I knew what lived inside them. Even when I knew what they wanted.

I came to believe a lot of them came from families where the Klan wasn't history, it was inheritance. Passed down quiet. Taught without being named. They denied it in public. In private, they fed it.

I could see it on their faces. The side looks when I said something they didn't like. The way jaws tightened. Once or twice, men stepped chest to chest with me and told me to stop preaching love for people who weren't like us. I told them everyone is like us. They couldn't see it. They'd been taught not to.

They soaked it all in. The slogans. The merch. The politics dressed up like sermons. I truly believe a lot of them had altars in their homes, but they weren't built for the God I preached. Turning people like that doesn't happen fast. It takes generations. Not moments.

Then people in our community started disappearing. Mostly Black and brown families. Quiet-like. Overnight. But some white folks vanished too. The ones who understood. The ones I wished I had more of in my pews.

A history professor from the local community college came to see me one afternoon. He was scared bad. His people had voted Democrat for generations. Folks knew who he was. He didn't go to rallies. Didn't wear the symbols. And that made him stand out. Made him dangerous. His kind always had been.

Then my congregation turned on me.

It was a Sunday like any other, or so it looked at first. The building was full. Every pew taken. But the air felt wrong. Tight. Like a storm sitting just outside the walls.

Right in the middle of the service, folks started standing up. One by one. Front pews first. Then the next. And the next. They didn't say a word. Just picked up their Bibles and walked out. No one looked back.

I was still preaching when the police came in.

They beat me where I stood. Right there in the house of God. They beat my wife, too. Not as bad as me, but bad enough. She never said a word. She'd been watching their faces for weeks. She knew what was coming long before I did.

They called me a lover of the Antichrist. I wasn't. I wanted democracy. I wanted things leveled out. I wanted folks to stop living with a hammer hanging over their heads every day.

They separated us.

They put me in a place where the floor stayed flooded so you couldn't lie down. Everything was wet. Cold. They laughed when they walked by, splashing through it with their boots like it was some kind of joke. There was no hiding. Just cages. Men packed in tight.

One man had every finger on his hand broken. Another was beaten again and again in places meant to shame him. The guards made sport of it. Like cruelty was something to pass the time.

I asked God where He was.

I didn't get an answer.

Nothing good came from that place.

I lost my church. I lost my faith.

And they killed my wife.

When they finally let us go, I made my way back to my little town. I didn't know who was who anymore. Couldn't tell what side anybody was on. The folks who helped put me in jail couldn't look me in the eye. They didn't look relieved. They looked empty. Hollowed out. Even with time passed, they still couldn't face what they'd been part of. They helped tear this country open. A rupture so deep it'll have a name someday. Mark my words.

I don't want the same Bible anymore. I don't want the same God I was handed. I want one that does something useful. One that shows up. One that helps people instead of standing back and watching them suffer.

My calling isn't here now.

The money's helped. I won't deny that. I'm back on my feet. Got clean clothes. Got a phone again. Got food to eat. Got vouchers for coffee in the mornings. I'm thankful for that. Truly. But when I walk through town, I feel their eyes on me. Always watching. They don't know what I went through. They don't know what they helped cause. But they wanted it. They cheered it on. Americans set against Americans, and they fed on it like it was gospel.

I can't look at them anymore.

They aren't part of my soul. They aren't part of anything good. They don't belong to God, not any God I recognize. I curse them under my breath, and I reckon I always will.

If I could speak to my congregation one last time, I wouldn't preach. I wouldn't plead. I'd walk out and I wouldn't come back.

Now we're on the other side of it. Things look hopeful on paper. Next week I'm taking a bus south. Mexico first. Then farther. And farther still. Till I don't feel the need to keep moving.

The checks go into a bank account now. I'll have a debit card. That gives me a chance to start over. Maybe I'll tend bar on a beach somewhere. Religion's finished for me. I might whistle a hymn now and then. Might lay a hand on somebody that's hurting. I liked that part of the work. I liked weddings. Not funerals.

I don't know the language where I'm headed. That'll be hard. Maybe I'll meet other Americans who left for the same reasons I did. But I won't preach. I won't even say I was a preacher.

If I'd done my job right, those people would've learned how to live without hate. Some folks never will. Some don't want to.

For now, the pressure's lifted. Love, if you wanna call it that, won in the end. I've got no love left for Alabama. I'm looking for a clean beginning.

I don't wanna talk about this again once I leave.

But I'll take my passport with me.

CHAPTER 19

COMMERCIAL REAL ESTATE AGENT
Atlanta, Georgia
Detained for not having her passport

I agreed to tell my story, but I ain't gonna look you in the eye while I do it. I'll sit right here with my coffee. That feels safer to me.

I was one of the top commercial real estate agents outside Atlanta. And I loved my job. Loved it the way some folks love music or church. I loved getting dressed up, loved talking business, loved walking into a room and knowing I belonged there. I liked helping people build something solid. Something real. I liked watching big ideas turn into square footage and signatures on a dotted line. I liked the money too. I'm not gonna lie about that. But it wasn't just the money.

I was made for that work.

Even as a little girl, I looked at buildings like they were alive. I'd stare at them and wonder who built them, who worked inside them, who owned them, who made the calls. I didn't want to be a nurse or a teacher or a flight attendant. I wanted to be the person who handed you the keys and said, here you go, this one's yours now.

I didn't have the words for it till high school. Rotary asked me what I wanted to be. Everybody else was saying doctor, lawyer, something respectable. I said I wanted to sell buildings. Some folks laughed. Some folks didn't. I got the scholarship anyhow.

I learned fast. Numbers made sense to me. Math always had. I took the tests. Passed them. Became an agent, then a broker. Before long I had people working under me. I closed million dollar deals. I mentored young agents who reminded me of myself. Every time a contract got signed, I felt that rush climb right up my chest. Not power. Not ego. Just forward motion. Like something good had clicked into place. That feeling never wore off.

Then things started to crack.

First time I got pulled over, they asked me for my passport. I honestly thought I'd misheard them. I had never left the United States. I lived in Atlanta. I worked in Atlanta. If I traveled, it was Vegas or Miami, not overseas. I didn't have any reason for a passport. Or so I thought.

They told me I needed one. On me. All the time.

That rattled me.

I gathered up every document they asked for. Birth certificate. Social Security card. Everything. I mailed it all in like I was told. That's what you're supposed to do when you believe the system still works.

Before anything came back, they stopped me again.

If you're American, prove it.

I told them my papers were already sent off. I showed them my license. That wasn't enough. By then people had already started disappearing around us. Folks who looked like me. Folks who worked hard and kept their heads down. I got scared in a way I had never been scared before. Not jumpy scared. Deep scared. The kind that settles in your bones and doesn't leave.

They yelled at me. Shook me. Slapped me down. Made me crawl right there on the ground. I could feel the hate rolling off them like heat off hot asphalt. Not because I'd done anything wrong. Just because I didn't have a piece of paper in my hand.

I begged them. I did. Told them to please let me get my mail. Told them my passport was coming any day now. I said it calm at first, then not so calm. Eventually they let me go. Not before they hurt me real good.

I went home crying so hard I couldn't catch my breath. Just sat there on the floor, shaking, trying to pull air back into my lungs.

I called everybody. Friends. Work people. Group chats. Facebook. Anybody who would answer. They'd taken my phone at first, then handed it back like nothing had happened. No video. No proof. Just my voice cracking while I tried to explain something that didn't even sound real when I said it out loud.

That's when it hit me.

They were watching me.

They knew my car. My license plate. My schedule. Every showing. Every appointment. Blacked-out SUVs started popping up everywhere I went. Parked across the street from properties I was supposed to sell. Just sitting there. Engines running. Watching. Like it was funny to them.

I was just trying to make it to the day my passport showed up.

It never did.

Then I got a call.

Man said his business was growing. Said he needed a big building. Over a million square feet. Asked if I could show it to him.

Of course I said yes. That was my job.

I pulled the listing. Went over the specs. Clean. Warehouse. Vacant close to a year. Solid opportunity. Nothing strange on paper. Nothing that would've made me hesitate.

I got dressed like I always did. Heels. Dress pressed. Hair done right. Nails checked. Lipstick just so. I loved that part. Still do, if I'm honest. That quiet moment where everything feels lined up and possible.

I got in my car feeling good. Blue sky everywhere. One of those Atlanta days that makes you think maybe things are finally settling down.

I was singing when I pulled up.

Then I saw the black cars.

One off to the side. Another across the way. Windows dark. Engines idling.

My stomach dropped straight through the floor.

That's when I knew.

That's when I knew.

I could hear the screaming before I even stepped out of my car. I could smell it too. That sour, burning stink that sticks in the back of your throat and won't let go. And all of it was coming from that million square foot warehouse I was supposed to lease.

They'd set me up.

One woman. By herself. That was the point. One man had his eye on me, and the rest were in on it. I didn't even get the chance to pretend otherwise. They let me step out of my car, real polite about it too. I knew I couldn't drive away. I was boxed in. Cars front and back. Doors already opening.

And there wasn't a damn thing I could do about it.

One of them smiled and said he wanted me to see something. Said he wanted me to walk the building. Wanted me to show him around proper. Like he was doing me some kind of favor. He squinted at me slow and mean. Big white man. Thick hands. Restless. Like they itched to touch something they hadn't earned.

I told him I had another appointment. Said I needed to go. Said it polite, the way women learn to say no without saying it.

I reached for my car door.

They stopped me.

I have replayed that moment more times than I can count. What I could have done different. I checked the listing. Checked the specs. Ran the numbers. The only thing I didn't do was get a referral. That was it. And even if I had, they would've found another way. Another trick. Another building. Another day.

The place wasn't empty. It was just empty online. They parked the cars around back. Tucked them out of sight. I didn't see them till it was too late. My instincts were already screaming before I even pulled in. That tight feeling in your chest you don't want to listen to. I should have turned around. It wouldn't have mattered.

I didn't have a gun. They did.
I had pepper spray. That was a joke.

Something hard pressed into my lower back. Metal. Cold. A gun. The man behind me had a soft Southern voice. Polite. Almost gentle. He was Black. That almost made it worse. It scrambled my head. Made it harder to understand what was happening.

Come on inside, he said.

I said no. I said my job was done here.

They told me it wasn't.

I tried not to cry. Tried to keep my knees from giving out. Tried to stand like I still had choices. I could hear the screaming clearer now, but I couldn't make out words. Just sounds. Women. Children. At first, my brain tried to save me. Told me it was a daycare nearby. Kids playing. Noise carrying on the air.

But there wasn't a single sound of joy in those voices.

Only terror.

They walked me forward. One on each side. One in front. One behind. The gun never left my back. I wet myself. I'm not ashamed to say that. Shame didn't survive that day.

It was a bright blue day. Too pretty. When they opened the door, my eyes couldn't adjust. The sunlight had been blinding. Inside was dark. Huge. Hollow. The air was thick. Wet. Like it had been breathed too many times already.

The first thing I thought was that it looked like a sculpture.

Cages stacked on cages on cages. Tall. Careful. Deliberate. Like one of those art pieces where you don't understand what you're seeing until it suddenly clicks. Bicycles piled into the shape of a bicycle.

Only this wasn't art.

This was cages.

I thought the floor was just covered. Blankets. Rags. Piles of things the mind tries to organize into objects so it doesn't have to call them people yet.

Then something moved.

Women, laid out shoulder to shoulder, knee to knee, like cargo that had shifted during transport. Some wrapped tight in thin blankets stiff with old spills. Some half-dressed. Some naked from the waist down. Children folded into them, clinging, fused by fear. Babies too quiet. Men stood behind the bars with sticks poking through, tapping, nudging, herding bodies that had already been reduced to shapes.

Some of the women made sounds I didn't recognize at first. Low. Protective. Not words. Not crying. Growling, like animals cornered too long. That's what they had been turned into.

Then they saw me.

It happened all at once. Heads lifting. Eyes locking. Mouths opening.

Run.
Run.
Run.

They screamed it until their voices shredded. They screamed knowing it wouldn't save me. Knowing what came after. They had seen it before. They were screaming anyway.

I didn't run.

I don't know why. There wasn't courage in it. Just a stillness. A decision made somewhere below thought. I lifted my head. That was the last thing I owned.

They shoved me into a cage. Metal on metal. The door slammed so hard my teeth clicked together. Someone laughed. Someone else said they'd be back later.

They were.

I stayed there for two years.

Time stopped behaving the way it's supposed to. Days blurred into hunger cycles. Nights into noise. Nobody told me if anyone looked for me. Nobody said my name. The outside world became a rumor that drifted in through guards' jokes and scraps of radio static.

When the doors finally opened, they didn't announce it. No orders. No speeches. They just shut off the lights and vanished.

Before we walked out, I finally saw how many of us there were.

Not dozens. Not hundreds.

Thousands.

I still don't understand how we didn't rise up together. How we didn't tear the place apart with our hands. But hunger makes you small. Fear makes you obedient. Exhaustion drains the will to imagine anything different. There were buckets for waste. Chains you stopped noticing. A smell so thick it became part of your skin.

When I stepped outside, my legs shook so bad I thought I'd fall.

But that's not what I noticed first.

Not the gray sky. Not how thin I'd become. Not the noise of other people crying and laughing and collapsing all at once.

It was the air.

Real air. Clean air. Not sour. Not rotting. Not soaked with human waste and breath and despair.

That first breath felt like a miracle.

Every breath still does.

Yes, we're all glad it's over.

But the air is what I remember most.

CHAPTER 20

No Passport Violation

West Virginia

My name is Cassandra Ruby Ruth Gertrude Suzanne Lee Sanchez

I have that many names because my five siblings were allowed to give me one middle name each at birth. I was the youngest. They each wanted to leave a mark on me.

My mother fled Honduras during the civil war. She arrived with nothing. Not even five dollars. Everything had been taken from her at one point or another. She told us those stories so we would know where we came from. She wanted us to understand what it meant to survive. We became naturalized citizens. She gave birth to all of us here. America was supposed to be the end of the running.

My father immigrated from Panama. They loved each other. That mattered. All they wanted was their family.

My dad worked as a janitor at the high school. My mother worked at a nursery, watering plants and keeping them alive so people would buy them.

We had just enough. We wore hand-me-downs and secondhand clothes, but we didn't care. At night we sang. My mother read us stories in Spanish. We learned our language. We had a good life.

Then, around 2014, things started to change. We were still in school. We tried not to notice. Everyone tried not to notice. Yes, we were on social media. I had a TikTok account. I talked about things. I was young.

I met a boyfriend. I got pregnant. It happened fast. I married him. I was barely eighteen. We loved each other. Seven months later our first baby came. Then another year passed and another baby came. We loved them both. We were getting by.

My mother helped when she could. My sisters helped. We could not afford daycare. I worked at a fast-food place I will not name because they were evil. My husband worked at a home improvement store. He was good at his job. His English was perfect. Mine was too.

I don't know how people knew we were Hispanic. We tried to fit in. Like, we did not bring tamales to work. We kept our heads down.

Then things got worse. You remember. One worse after another worse after another worse. People in our community were picked up early on. They just vanished. No explanations. Then doors started getting knocked down. Then it could happen anywhere. On the street. In a car. In the grocery store.

If you did not have your passport or whatever papers they wanted that day, they took you. It did not matter. They were filling quotas.

Life became unbearable. My mother warned us. Don't go on social media. Don't say your name. We made plans. What to grab. Where to go. Where to meet. We talked through every possibility. One ear on the news. One ear trying to block it out. That was life for anyone with Spanish heritage.

One day, I came home from work. I went to pick up my babies from my mother's house. The house was empty. My babies were gone. My family was gone.

I screamed. Not just for my children. For everyone. What are you supposed to do? Call 911 and say your family has been disappeared? You cannot do that.

There was a number someone gave out. They said it could help. I think it was a trap. I called. I said I was at my mother's house. I said my children were gone. My family was gone.

Less than ten minutes later, they came. Lights on. Sirens. Like they had been waiting around the corner. They took me.

I screamed. I kicked at their shins. They pinned me harder. The more I fought, the worse it got. They pulled my hair. Punched my stomach. Kicked me. Hit my face. Men in heavy uniforms beating a woman who barely weighed one hundred and twenty pounds.

All I could do was cry for my babies. For my husband. For my family.

They took me away. I never saw any of them again.

Three years passed. I still don't know where they are. I have never found them.

We were hardworking, taxpaying citizens. I was born here. My children were born here. We belonged here.

Dark hair. Dark eyes. Brown skin. That was enough.

Nothing has been right since that day. Nothing makes me happy. Yes, I am glad it's over. Yes, it has ended.

But what do you do with people like me who lost everything?

The money they give me does not matter.

Nothing replaces a family.

CHAPTER 21

Housing Coordinator
New York City

I keep a spreadsheet. That's how it starts and ends for me.

Green means available. Yellow means pending inspection. Red means don't assign. Red used to mean mold or fire damage or unsafe wiring. Now it mostly means history.

The homes are fine. Structurally. Roofs intact. Plumbing works. Most of them still have curtains. Some still have dishes in the cabinets. I don't inventory personal items anymore. That was changed after the first month.

We are instructed to call them "vacated residences." Not seized. Not cleared. Vacated.

People ask me if the houses belonged to someone before.

I say yes.

They ask if they are allowed to move things.

I say yes.

They ask if anyone will come back for them.

I say no.

That part is not in the script, but it's accurate.

I match families to houses based on size and proximity to services. Trauma proximity is not a metric we have been given. Neither is grief compatibility. I place a woman who spent two years in a cage into a home where children's height marks are still penciled on the doorframe. I don't point them out. She sees them anyway.

Some people cry. Some people don't go inside right away. One man slept on the porch for three nights. He said the house breathed differently at night.

I document that he declined indoor shelter temporarily.

We are told not to remove photos unless requested. We are told memory is personal property. We are told continuity helps healing.

I don't know who wrote that sentence.

Sometimes a former neighbor comes by. They stand at the curb. They say things like, "I wondered what would happen to this place."

I say, "It has been reassigned."

They nod like that answers something.

I get paid every two weeks. I am efficient. My supervisor says I am compassionate because I don't rush people through the keys.

At the end of the day, I lock my filing cabinet. I leave the lights on in the hallway because some residents prefer it. I don't think about who slept in those rooms before. That is not part of my job.

CHAPTER 22

Clerk, Intake Division
Philadelphia

I sat at Station 14.

My stamp says APPROVED in blue ink. The blue runs sometimes. We are waiting on new pads.

People slide documents under the glass. Some hands shake. Some hands are very still. Still hands are harder. Still hands mean they have already learned waiting.

I verify identity. That has become ironic. I don't comment on it.

If the form is complete, I stamp it. If a not complete, I slide it back and tell them what is missing. Birth certificates are often missing. Death certificates are more often missing.

There is a box to check for "family status unknown."

That box used to be rare.

Now, it's common.

I don't ask follow-up questions unless required. That rule keeps things moving. Efficiency was the word in the last memo. Compassion slows throughput.

Some people thank me. I don't respond. We are not supposed to engage beyond procedure.

Once, a woman asked me if the address I approved used to belong to someone else.

I said yes.

She asked if they were alive.

I said I don't have access to that information.

That was true.

When I stamp a file, it makes a sound. It's a good sound. Final. I like that part. People like that part too. They relax when they hear it.

APPROVED.

It does not mean safe. It does not mean whole. It does not mean justice.

It means the line is finished.

At five o'clock, I place the stamp in the drawer. I wash my hands. The ink comes off easily.

Tomorrow, I will approve more lives.

CHAPTER 23

Accountant
Colorado

I don't clap.
I don't cry.
I don't do the big exhale like everybody else who just ran a marathon and crossed the finish line holding hands.

You wanna know what I did when they said it was over?

I checked the exits.

I've been right too many times to pretend this is the end.
I saw the math early.
I read the footnotes nobody wanted to read.
I listened when the tone shifted, when language started doing that slippery thing where words mean less and power means more.

I was there.
Not the front row with the flags and the chants and the dopamine.
I was there in the crowd behind the crowd.
The part that knows when to move and when to vanish.

The Pendulum Swings Back

You call it a mob like it's a cartoon.
Like we were all the same.
We weren't.

Some people were drunk on it.
Some people were scared.
Some people were hunting.
Some people were just trying not to be the next body with no plaque.

I watched it turn.
I watched neighbors get loud.
I watched silence become currency.
I watched smart people start talking stupid because stupid was safer.

And yeah, I survived.
That doesn't mean I'm grateful.
It means I learned where to hide my mouth.

Now they say it's over.
They say calm down.
They say rebuild.
They say look, the lights are back on, the shelves are full, the markets are breathing again.

Of course they are.
That's how the reset works.

You gotta get the taxes flowing again.
You gotta get people shopping again.

You gotta get everybody tired enough to mistake relief for justice.

This isn't peace.
This is a truce with a timer.

I don't trust quiet.
Quiet is how it started.

I don't trust apologies without names.
I don't trust money without memory.
I don't trust systems that say "never again" but keep the tools on the shelf.

You think I'm angry?

Good.
Anger means my nerve endings still work.

I'm not breaking windows.
I'm not lighting torches.
I'm watching.
I'm cataloging.
I'm remembering who smiled and who looked away and who suddenly can't remember a damn thing.

Because that swing you're talking about?
That pendulum?

It never stops.
It just pauses long enough for people to forget where it was headed.

So yeah, I know it's over.

I also know what comes next.

And this time, I'm not pretending I didn't see it coming. Keep your eyes open, it will happen again. They learned but so did we.

END HERE

This book ends here.
The events described don't end here.

The individuals whose voices appear in these pages were released, relocated, compensated, or classified as survivors. Those actions resolved immediate liability. They did not resolve the cause.

Records remain incomplete.
Some names were never recovered.
Some bodies were never identified.
Some orders were signed without explanation and remain sealed.

Financial restitution was issued where possible.
Housing was reassigned where available.
Medical and psychological services were offered on a temporary basis.

None of these actions restores what was taken.

There has been no comprehensive accounting of how authority was expanded, who authorized it, or how compliance was normalized. There has been no universal agreement on when the line was crossed, only that it was.

This period is now referred to as "over."
That designation is procedural.

Systems that enabled these events remain operational.

Personnel who executed orders were often reassigned, not removed.

Language has softened. Policies have been renamed.

Public attention has shifted.

History shows that recovery does not prevent recurrence. It only shortens memory.

The responsibility for what follows does not belong to the people in this book alone. It belongs to those who read it and decide what is acceptable next.

No further statements will be issued at this time.

Final Note

At the time of publication, not all cases referenced in this book have been resolved.

Some names remain unknown.
Some records remain sealed.
Some locations remain unmarked.

This book ends here.
The record does not.

About the Author

Sugar Gay Isber McMillan is an author and journalist whose work explores resilience, human behavior, and the moments that test who we are. She has written nearly eighty books across fiction and nonfiction, blending narrative storytelling with clear-eyed observation of the world around us.

Her work often focuses on people navigating upheaval, change, and recovery, with an emphasis on voice, empathy, and survival. In addition to her writing, she has spent decades working in media, education, and creative industries.

Readers can explore more of her books, projects, and upcoming releases by visiting the QR code included here.

Scan the code to see more books on Amazon by Sugar Gay Isber McMillan.

www.ingramcontent.com/pod-product-compliance
Lightning Source LLC
Chambersburg PA
CBHW050454110426
42743CB00017B/3361